# CONTENTS

# A CULTURE OF SERVICE

# INTRODUCTION

*"How can our organization become*
*great at customer service?"*

That is the question that many people are asking today. My response is: "The process of becoming world class in customer service is a difficult journey and requires much more than an occasional speech or a program of the year."

When someone asks you to think of a company in a particular industry that is known for excellent customer service, most people have a hard time thinking of more than one.

There are some organizations that may gain temporary success in this area, but soon fall back to mediocrity. The majority of companies in business today have a goal of delivering excellent service to their customers.

Why is it, then, that when I mention to a group of people that I consult with companies on customer service, they are quick to give me a list of organizations that need my services?

The answer is: Becoming excellent in customer service and sustaining that over a long period of time is hard work!

Year after year, many companies roll out their customer service programs of the year or bring in well-known speakers to motivate their troops. Very few companies understand that reaching this desired level of service requires a change in culture and successful implementation of many processes.

Why is it important for companies to change their culture? With modern technology, it takes longer for your competition to change their culture than it does to replicate your product or service. We have entered what I call an "Age of Commodities" and there is more competition now than ever. If your competition is not across the street, then your customers can purchase products from your competitor on the Internet.

With all the competition and ease of duplicating products, the only way one company can distinguish itself from the competition is by every employee providing excellent customer service. People will continue to buy from those they trust and with whom they share a relationship.

Another reason to provide excellent customer service is that unhappy customers talk! You have all had a bad experience somewhere and made it your mission in life to tell everyone you know about the company. The average unhappy customer will tell at least nine people about their bad experience, and the secondhand conversations can be damaging to your bottom line.

The mission of this book is to help leaders and employees at all levels begin the process of creating a culture of service. We will discuss topics from accountability to teamwork and from respecting the client to measuring your success. The final chapter is dedicated to helping you hold on once you reach the top.

Once you have implemented many of the items discussed in the early chapters, your customers will begin to notice a change, but so will your competitors. Know that they will try hard to copy what you have done, but a positive culture of service is difficult to duplicate!

One definition of culture is the combination of behaviors, actions and attitudes that define an organization or group of people.

What behaviors define your culture? Do your employees at all levels spring into action when there is a high demand for services, or do they continue at a normal, relaxed pace?

What attitudes characterize the way your front-line employees think about their customers? Do they show respect to your customers, even when they are not present, or do your employees joke about a recent customer interaction?

The great companies and organizations that are known for consistently delivering excellent service have invested a lot of time and other resources to ensure each employee does not have to be reminded of the standard of service every day. It is second nature! They know what to do in different circumstances and act the same way whether or not their supervisor is watching.

That only happens when you create a culture of service!

# A CULTURE OF SERVICE

# 1 TAKE CARE OF THE SMALL THINGS

Creating a culture of service requires that you do a lot of things consistently right and develop attitudes that govern the behaviors of all your employees. One of the attitudes that is very important is being diligent in dealing with the smallest details of your operation.

A close friend of mine, David Dennis, would frequently say:

"If you make a big deal out of little things,
then the little things won't become a big deal!"

There are many managers and leaders who have mistakenly confused being involved in the details of their company or department with micromanaging. These are two totally different concepts. One of the challenges with organizations providing exceptional customer service today is that the leadership is too far removed from regular contact with their customers.

You may also have heard a manager make the following statement:

"I don't need to get involved in the details.
That's why I hired all these employees."

While it is true that a leader does not have the time to know every detail and every task others perform, they must possess the ability to quickly identify problem areas. Once these areas are identified, they must drill down to the level of detail necessary to understand the problem, put their finger on the root cause and find a solution to the issue.

For those in a leadership role, this starts by knowing the right questions to ask. The first few times you start asking questions of those in your department, you may receive some negative reactions. This can be perceived by some people that you are micromanaging them or that you do not trust what they are doing.

Over time, your employees will realize that you are simply doing your job and ensuring everyone is delivering services to a high standard. They will become less defensive and learn to be ready for your requests. This also helps the leader remain connected to his or her employees.

To avoid crossing the line into the land of micromanagement, leaders should delegate the resolution of problems instead of feeling that they need to personally perform every detailed task necessary to resolve each problem.

Let's look at an example:

> Sara is a mid-level manager at a telecommunications company. She is responsible for managing existing customers in a five-state region. The fifth of every month she receives an account activity report. This report has several sections, but one area gives the sales activity for the top 10 accounts in each state.
>
> In July, Sara was looking through the report as she did every month. This time she noticed that the total sales activity was down significantly in New Jersey, one of her five states. She was

located in Pennsylvania and did not spend a lot of time in the New Jersey office.

Sara picked up the phone and called the territory manager responsible for the New Jersey accounts. The manager, Jim, was expecting the call and had a careful response prepared. Jim informed Sara that everything was fine. "We are just experiencing a normal slowdown for this time of year," he replied when questioned.

This is where the moment of truth occurs. Some less-experienced leaders would let it go and simply accept this explanation and wait to review the numbers next month.

Not Sara. She had been around awhile and immediately decided this was an area that warranted a closer look. She informed Jim that she would like to pay a visit to his office next week. Jim was instructed to have detailed account activity reports ready to review.

The next week Sara arrived and began reviewing the reports. There was one client who had historically accounted for a large portion of the New Jersey business. This client's purchases were one-third what they normally were during a typical month.

Sara probed further. Jim did not have an explanation. Sara decided to bring in the account manager who was over this particular client and have a meeting in the office. After just five minutes, it was clear that this account manager had something to hide.

Sara and Jim then called the client to set up a meeting at the client's office. During this visit, the client explained how the account manager had been caught falsifying some information on a recent bill. The client decided to take their business to the competing firm in town.

After some quick apologizing and a termination and re-assignment of account managers, they were able to save this important client.

Sara's skill of evaluating data and then knowing how to ask the right questions until she got to the bottom of the issue was the difference that retained this client. It also let her staff know that they were going to be held accountable for their performance.

## Details ... Beyond Leadership

It is not only leaders who must have a passion for details, but employees at every level in an organization must see the value in doing even the smallest task with excellence. Great organizations are built on the shoulders of employees who do their assigned tasks with precision and passion. This includes the janitor cleaning the floors to the executive negotiating a big deal. Each person can positively or negatively impact a customer's experience by the way he or she greets a guest or follows through on a commitment.

In dealing with customers, you never know when you are about to press one of their hot buttons. What seems like a small, insignificant thing to you may be a major issue to them. It may also be the final straw that tips them over the edge into what may appear as irrational behavior.

If an employee develops the attitude to take every task seriously and to perform at a high level of competence, they will have fewer major problems with which to deal.

# CULTURE CORNERSTONES

## WHAT?

☐ *Develop a culture that views every task as important, no matter the size or perceived value to the organization.*

## HOW?

☐ *Create the expectation that any detail, no matter how small, may be reviewed at any time. This is not micromanaging, but solid leadership.*

☐ *Positive reinforcement and praise should be used hand in hand with coaching and discipline.*

## BENEFIT?

☐ *The team members at all levels will be diligent and strive toward performing their jobs with excellence, not out of fear, but because it is the right thing to do.*

☐ *Problems, especially customer issues, are much less costly to solve when they are caught early before the customer is lost or extensive recovery is needed.*

# A CULTURE OF SERVICE

# 2 | GREAT SERVICE STARTS WITHIN

In every organization, there are members of the team who interface directly with end customers, who ultimately buy your product or service. For these team members to be effective and offer a high level of service, they must have support from the rest of the team. There will always be employees who rarely have contact with the end customer.

Their jobs are to provide support services. Their ability to perform with excellence is just as important as having a top-rated sales force. (Let's call these groups "internal departments.") Many organizations spend most of their efforts providing customer-service training for the departments that deal directly with the end customer. This is important, but the internal departments must also understand the importance of customer service.

Let's look at some examples of internal departments.

## Information Technology

With the increasing importance of technology in every aspect of our society, most organizations rely heavily on their Information Technology Departments. Coming from a background in technology, I know that a common problem is the feeling of superiority among the staff and leadership due to their specialized technical knowledge.

Leadership must constantly reinforce the concept of internal customer service. The Information Technology employees must strive to communicate in terms that will be understood by their non-technical internal customers. They must adopt the attitude that they are there to serve the other departments and offer the tools necessary for them to provide excellent service to the end customers.

This should not be interpreted in any way that they are less important than the departments they serve. In a healthy organization, there is a mutual respect between departments and a realization that it is essential for everyone to perform their jobs to the highest standards in order for the end customer to be satisfied.

## Accounting/Purchasing

Another internal department is the Accounting Department, including the purchasing function. Even though many employees in this department may have interactions with end customers, their primary customer groups are internal.

One twist to the services provided by the Accounting Department is that they are commonly asked to hold other departments accountable for ethical financial operations. In doing so, there may be times when they have to enforce company policies and report improper actions. Even in this difficult role, they can still have a customer service attitude when confronting other team members. Too often, employees use these opportunities to exert their authority over others in order to boost their own feelings of worth and importance.

This is not to say that they should not take their responsibilities seriously, but there are ways to hold others accountable while making them feel like partners.

## Internal Feedback

Exceptional companies often solicit feedback from end customers through tools such as surveys. It is just as important for departments to gather feedback from their internal customers. This can be accomplished by adding a few questions to the annual employee survey for employees to rate the level of service they receive from internal departments.

Employees in internal departments will deliver a high level of customer service if they know that the employees in the other departments will most likely provide feedback on their performance. Surveying these fellow employees creates a feeling that they should be treated as customers.

Once this feedback is received, the leadership team of the internal departments should use the data to create an action plan that focuses attention on the areas of weakness. This plan should be shared with their internal customers, and regular progress updates should be given.

One word of caution! If you are going to go through the effort of asking others to take the time to give you their opinion, make sure you respond and demonstrate that you hear their feedback. If you have no intention of making changes based on the information that comes back from a survey, don't waste everyone's time.

All employees should treat their co-workers as if they were paying customers. This includes returning phone calls and e-mails in a timely manner. Do you find yourself changing the tone of your voice depending on whether you are talking with someone from another department or an external customer? If so, this may be an indication that you are not treating your co-workers as customers.

If you happen to be in a leadership role, the employees in your group are, to a certain degree, customers. Yes, you are there to hold them accountable, but you are also there to remove any obstacles that prevent them from accomplishing their assigned tasks. Every leader's review should include feedback from those they supervise.

## Defining a Customer

Employees in internal support departments must develop the mindset that the colleagues they serve are their customers. When possible, all employees should have the opportunity to visit the workplace of the people they support. This means that if you work in payroll, you should take the time to visit the different business units you support. It does not have to be a lengthy process, but simply an opportunity to see your co-workers in action in their environments.

If you work in a computer support center, you should try to understand the challenges that the sales teams face when attempting to use their laptop computers and sales software.

Understanding the bigger picture of why the organization exists will instill a sense of purpose in some jobs that can become routine.

## Final Thought ...

Why is internal customer service so important? What does it have to do with the customer service your paying clients will receive? It can be very tiring to have to shift the way we think and behave depending on who is in front of us or on the other end of the phone!

If you develop a culture where all interactions are done with respect, you don't have to worry about the day when you forget to switch gears and accidentally treat an end customer poorly.

# CULTURE CORNERSTONES

## WHAT?

❏ *Develop a culture where internal customer service is practiced.*

## HOW?

❏ *Train internal departments on customer service, just as you would the groups that represent your organization to the paying customer.*

❏ *Give all employees the opportunity to rate and provide feedback in the internal departments. This can be done as part of an annual employee survey or integrated into a group's continuous improvement process.*

❏ *Once the feedback has been collected, DO SOMETHING WITH IT! Within 30 days of the end of a formal survey, the internal team should have identified the opportunities for improvement and created a detailed action plan to improve service to their customers.*

## BENEFIT?

❏ *The employees serving in an internal role will develop a greater sense of worth as they understand how their work impacts others in the company.*

❏ *The team members in outward-facing positions will be able to perform their jobs with excellence. This will result in satisfied customers!*

# 3 | TRAINING AND DEVELOPMENT

**G**reat customer service organizations have a culture that values the training and development of their employees! It all starts before employees have their first day on the job. A candidate interviewing for a job has already made some initial opinions about what is important to the potential employer based on how employees conduct themselves during the interview process.

## Orientation

Once an employee shows up for their first day with the company, that employee MUST receive training as part of a new-employee orientation program. This can vary from company to company, but every organization should have some sort of orientation program. Unfortunately, many companies have turned their orientation session into a time to complete benefits paperwork. It is much more than that!

Prior to a new employee representing you in front of your customers, they should clearly understand customer service expectations and have a basic knowledge of the different products or services offered by the company. This is the one opportunity to set clear expectations.

Too many companies use on-the-job training for everything, and throw employees into the daily operation without providing the basics.

The habits formed during the first six weeks on a job will be difficult to break. Not every co-worker, although they may be a good employee, is qualified to teach new workers the details of the job or the culture you desire to establish.

## Job-Specific Training

Every job has specific responsibilities and tasks that go with the territory. Some positions may not require a significant amount of advanced training prior to the employees being left to perform their duties. For others, especially where there are safety or liability issues, it is important that the new employees be thoroughly trained, and possibly even certified, in their positions.

Most organizations tend to put job-specific training in the category of "on-the-job" training. Although there is a valid place for this in most occupations, more often than not, the employees are thrown into the position because the organization has not taken the time to develop any formal training.

## Soft-skill Training

Recent graduates joining the work force may have received adequate technical or occupation-specific training, but it is rare to find someone who has received training in the "soft-skill" areas. Soft-skills refer to topics such as:

- ❖ Communication: Speaking and Listening Skills
- ❖ Leadership
- ❖ Conflict Resolution
- ❖ Effective Meeting Facilitation
- ❖ Win-Win Negotiation

Organizations, and their customers, will benefit when all employees receive the appropriate training in these areas. These skills are crucial to their success but are usually only learned through bad experiences.

## Ongoing Development/Continuing Education

Training, just like improving business processes, is a never-ending challenge. One of the motivating factors mentioned in employee satisfaction surveys is that their employer continues to invest in their development and professional education.

## Mentoring

This category of training is rarely done effectively. Some organizations may have a formal process to assign new employees to a more-seasoned mentor. The problem is that they fail to train the mentor in how to take this investment in time and turn it into a meaningful activity. Most mentoring programs end up as simply checking in on the new employee periodically. As time goes on, everyone becomes busy with their daily tasks and these get-togethers are less and less frequent, until they disappear entirely.

Simple checklists, like the one on the following page, can add some structure to a mentoring program and help both participants realize the intended improvement in their ability and performance.

# Mentor Program Checklist

Mentor name: _____

Name of person being mentored: _____

Date of meeting: _____

Significant area(s) of discussion and future effort:

_____

_____

_____

_____

*Action Steps*

**Target date**　　**Task or activity**

_____　　_____

_____　　_____

_____　　_____

Challenges during the next 30 days:

_____

_____

_____

_____

Next meeting date and location:

_____

Even though the "official" purpose of a mentoring program is to transfer knowledge and experience to new employees or leaders, if done correctly, the mentor usually benefits as much or more than the one being mentored. The process helps refocus the skills of the mentor.

## Cross Training

This form of training should be just as intentional as the others, although it is normally absent from most organizations. When new employees join your organization, prior to having them start their full-time positions, it would be helpful if they spent some time in each of the major departments. This gives them a well-rounded feel for the activities of each area and will help them know where to go if either they or a customer need assistance.

The time spent observing other positions does not have to take weeks, just a few days during the orientation period would be time well spent.

For existing employees, a program should be established to give each employee half a day each quarter to spend with someone in another department. If a group routinely provides services for another department, it would be a good idea for them to spend time observing operations of the internal customer.

## Summary

Having a complete training program can have a significant impact on customer service. Everyone has had the unfortunate experience of interacting with a salesperson or other employee who has not been properly trained for their position.

If this happens to be the first contact a customer has with an organization, having a negative encounter with an untrained employee can encourage customers to search for a company with properly trained employees, leading them directly to your competitor.

# CULTURE CORNERSTONES

## WHAT?

❑ *Create a culture that values learning!*

## HOW?

❑ *Develop a master training plan for each member of the organization. This should include job specific training, crosstraining, soft-skill training and continued education.*

❑ *Create a formal mentoring program. This program can vary by position, but should have some structure and accountability.*

## BENEFIT?

❑ *Individuals who have a thirst for knowledge will deliver better customer service and be more valuable employees.*

❑ *Properly trained employees make fewer mistakes, reducing the chance of upsetting a customer, having to repeat a task, or replace a product.*

❑ *Employers who invest in training create a work environment with high morale and low turnover.*

# 4 | EMPLOYMENT EMPOWERMENT

**W**hat does this phrase really mean? It has been used in books and business training seminars for years, yet very few organizations have figured out how to put it into practice. One thing it does not mean is for leadership to hand over their responsibility to make decisions and guide the company or department. Empowerment does not mean that employees have free reign to do as they see fit without any boundaries or policies to follow.

How many times have you approached a clerk or front-line staff member and offered a criticism or suggestion on how their company could improve and better meet your needs? If you are like me, the response you receive, more often than not, would sound something like this:

"You are not the first person to suggest that. If *they* would do that, it would make my life easier, too. That is all handled at the corporate headquarters. We don't have a say about that at our store."

When I hear a response like that, I know I have run into an organization that does not understand what it means to empower their employees.

Unfortunately, the senior leadership in most organizations is several levels removed from having direct contact with the customers. It is the front-line employees who have the interaction, yet we have stripped them of the ability to do anything when they come across an opportunity to make things better.

**Empowering employees has three main components:**

1. **Eyes & Ears**
2. **Hands & Feet**
3. **Heart & Mind**

## Eyes & Ears

Employees at every level of an organization must understand that they each can be the point of entry for a major improvement in the way business is conducted or a product is designed. For this to happen, they must have a method of submitting this feedback or suggestions to the appropriate person to make something happen.

It is not uncommon for a new employee to be performing their job and then identify an opportunity for improvement. Most people start a position with the goal of doing a good job and making a difference. They may mention their idea to a supervisor who would respond with, "Thanks, John. I'll take care of it. You can get back to your work now."

Weeks go by and the same particular problem occurs over and over and several customers complain. John, still relatively new with the company, has a positive attitude and says to the customer, "Thanks for bringing that to my attention. We are working on that and it should be corrected soon."

After giving that response a dozen times and seeing no signs of any action from his supervisor or others who have the power to fix the problem, John becomes discouraged. The next time a customer brings up the issue, John gives the response mentioned earlier. He has distanced himself from the "company" and has lost any feeling of being empowered.

So how do you keep this from happening?

- **Train Your Leaders.** From the top to the first-line supervisor, make sure your leadership team knows how to document suggestions and pass them on to the correct person who can properly evaluate the idea and take action if needed.

- **Take Action.** Make sure your organization does not get so big and hard to maneuver.

- **Close the Loop with the Employee.** Make sure the employee who brought the suggestion forth knows what happened with the idea. If it is not something that is going to be implemented, let them know that the idea was considered and give them an explanation of why no change was made.

- **Share the Credit.** If a suggestion results in a positive change or product improvement, give credit to the employee who made the suggestion. It is amazing how a little positive recognition will motivate any employee and keep the ideas flowing.

## Hands & Feet

When most people think of empowerment, they associate the term with giving employees the authority to make decisions and do what is needed to resolve a situation. In addition to encouraging an employee to listen, observe and pass on an idea, it is critical that they also have the ability to do something about customer complaints or suggestions.

Let me give you an illustration of this point:

A while back, my family and I were eating at a restaurant near our home in Orlando. It was part of a large national chain of table service restaurants serving a variety of foods. My daughter ordered a kid's meal with macaroni & cheese. As far as these meals go, this was relatively expensive. The meal came and it consisted of a small bowl of macaroni & cheese (easily recognized as the one in the blue box) and a drink.

I asked my server if that was all that came with this meal. She replied that it was just the macaroni & cheese and a drink. I asked her if there was any way she could add a small cup of grapes from their salad bar. The waitress was polite, but informed me that she was not allowed to do that. I asked to visit with her manager.

The manager of the restaurant came to our table, and I explained my request again. He apologized for the situation, but then proceeded to tell me that he was not authorized to add the dozen grapes to our meal. The menus were set at corporate headquarters, and they are not allowed to deviate from those menus in even the slightest way.

Does that example sound ridiculous to you? Unfortunately, it is very common. Here you had the manager of this entire restaurant, and he was not even empowered to give a customer a few grapes to respond to a complaint and satisfy a regular customer.

This particular problem went all the way to the leadership at their corporate headquarters. Often, this occurs because someone feels that they are more qualified to make this type of decision than those who are in the field interacting with the customers every day. If I were that manager, I would not feel challenged if I did not have the ability to make even a simple decision.

One the other hand, we have all heard the stories of successful organizations like the Ritz Carlton Hotel where every employee is empowered to take the steps necessary to resolve a guest problem. While I was working at Walt Disney World, from the initial training called "Traditions," every employee was trained that once they were made aware of a guest problem, it was their responsibility to work with the other "Cast Members" (this is what Disney calls their employees) to resolve the problem.

## Heart & Mind

The third part of creating a culture where your employees feel empowered deals with the heart and mind. The best organizations have figured out how to make even their entry-level employees feel a sense of pride and ownership for what goes on at the company.

This is partially accomplished by making sure every employee understands the important role they play as the eyes, ears, hands and feet of the organization. As mentioned above, giving each employee a process to communicate complaints, suggestions and even positive feedback to the right person not only provides a great source of ideas for improvement, but it also helps employees feel that they can make a difference.

As a friend of mine, Lee Colan says in his book, *Passionate Performance: Engaging Minds and Hearts to Conquer the Competition,* "The first strategy to fulfill this need is to involve your employees in defining and improving their work processes. Clearly defined processes are critical to any efficient operation. Even in the most routine jobs, you can still get input from employees about ways to make improvements. When you give team members the appropriate level of autonomy, you engage their minds. The benefit to you? People support what they help create. When employees support the process, they are much more likely to give discretionary effort."

**True leadership is all about learning to work through others, not doing everything yourself.**

If you are a leader and have a hard time giving others in your organization responsibility and the authority that goes with it, you might want to consider finding a new role for yourself. True leadership is all about learning to work through others, not doing everything yourself. Organizations whose leadership team understands how to empower their employees will far outperform those that have a heavy-handed, top-down style of management.

# CULTURE CORNERSTONES

## WHAT?

☐ *Develop a culture that empowers every part of an employee: Eyes, Ears, Hands, Feet, Heart and Mind.*

## HOW?

☐ *Develop processes and communication channels to allow any employee to relay customer feedback or suggestions.*

☐ *Train leadership to delegate the appropriate level of authority to employees.*

☐ *Gather employee feedback, suggestions and ideas for improving products or services through the use of annual employee surveys.*

## BENEFIT?

☐ *Employees who are truly empowered are more challenged and love their work.*

☐ *Leaders who learn to delegate can leverage their knowledge and skills.*

☐ *Customers are pleasantly surprised when a front-line employee actually cares and has the ability to solve their problem.*

# CUSTOMER FEEDBACK LOOP

**5**

In order for any organization to avoid becoming stale, it must have a set of processes in place that make up the "Customer Feedback Loop." Notice, it is not called the "Customer Feedback Line." The difference between a line and a loop is that a line has a definite starting and ending; whereas, a loop denotes a continuous process.

Every time you take a trip around the loop, you should be dealing with smaller and less-significant issues. This allows a company to constantly raise the bar on product and service quality, while having a well-tuned process in place to deal with the occasional major issue that is bound to surface.

Listen to Customer Feedback & Measure

Prioritize problems and identify trends

Respond & Recover as needed

Adjust product or service

Let's take a look at the four major components of a customer feedback loop:

### 4 Stages of a Customer Feedback Loop:

1. Listen to Customer Feedback & Measure
2. Prioritize Problems & Identify Trends
3. Respond & Recover as Needed
4. Adjust the Product, Service or Personnel

## Listen to Customer Feedback & Measure

The first step in the loop is to listen to your customers. Feedback may be gathered using several methods, each with its own positives and negatives:

❖ Comment Cards
  • Very small percent of responses; mostly negative
  •Provides an opportunity for customers to express themselves

❖ Informal Interviews
  • Balanced feedback, although many customers will avoid confrontation

❖ Focus Groups
  • Difficult to arrange with end customers
  • May be useful when meeting with partners and internal customers

❖ Employees
  • Listen to the front-line employees; they often know how to improve your services

Keep in mind that when you are soliciting feedback, you may receive comments and criticism that are not always accurate or justified. That is where the next step comes into play.

## Prioritize Problems & Identify Trends

When you have data from many sources, it can become overwhelming if you do not have a process in place to analyze the data. Feedback can be sorted into the following categories:

- ❖ Major concern – Something would fall into this category if a problem comes to your attention that meets one of the following criteria:
  - There is a major safety or health risk involved with the product, service or process
  - The problem occurred with one of your key clients or customers
  - There is a potential for a significant financial loss if the problem is not corrected quickly

- ❖ Customer complaint or suggestion that appears to be valid and is worthy of a response or recovery to satisfy a customer

- ❖ General or anonymous complaints or suggestions

- ❖ Positive feedback regarding a product, service or employee

Once the feedback has been "triaged" and divided into one of the categories above, you can begin the "Respond & Recover" step that is discussed next.

Not all individual problems require an immediate response, but every complaint, suggestion or problem should be entered into a database system. On a monthly basis, feedback reports should be run to organize and count the items in each of the major categories, regions or business units.

This will allow the company to identify trends and common issues that, when dealt with and solved individually, don't seem to be of major concern.

Let me give an example of what frequently happens when organizations fail to take this important step.

> One Christmas season, I went into our regular grocery store to purchase some items for a party we were having. After searching for a particular item that is popular during the holiday season, I finally asked a store manager. He was very friendly and gave me the following response:
>
> "I apologize for running out of that item. I have been here for eight years, and I believe that we have run out of that particular thing every year at this time."
>
> If this store had a process in place to analyze common problems and document trends, they would have realized that they needed to increase the order level of this item as the holiday season approached.

Once you have your process in place to organize your feedback and spot trends, you will be able to avoid repeating the same mistakes year after year.

## Respond & Recover as Needed

The third part of the customer feedback loop is to respond to the customer and recover so you retain them as your customer. Not every customer comment, complaint or suggestion demands a response, but if the problem falls into the category of "Major Concerns," there is a strong possibility that if you don't acknowledge the customers' complaints, they may find somewhere else to take their business.

Chapter 7 deals with the topic of "Guest Recovery," which discusses the aspects of recovering when something goes wrong.

## Adjust the Product, Service or Personnel

Very few organizations ever implement the fourth step in the customer feedback loop. Some companies get to the process of organizing their customer feedback, but that is where it stops. In the prior example about the grocery store, the proper way to respond to the data that showed them running out of an item every holiday season would be to put a reminder in place so that the order level was increased for that time the next year.

It is a waste for companies to go through the effort and expense to solicit feedback from customers and then not use that valuable information to improve the products and services or make personnel adjustments.

# CULTURE CORNERSTONES

## WHAT?

☐ *Create a COMPLETE customer feedback loop.*

## HOW?

☐ *Form a work team to look at each of the four steps in the customer feedback loop. This works best if you include employees from each major department and at various levels within the organization.*

☐ *Develop the details for each step in the loop and train all employees on the new processes and procedures.*

## BENEFIT?

☐ *Once this culture cornerstone is firmly in place in an organization, a desire to continuously improve in every area will become part of the culture.*

☐ *Costly errors in product or service delivery will be reduced when a balanced set of measurements is utilized.*

☐ *Customers become very loyal when they see their feedback acted upon and the products or services move closer to meeting their needs.*

# 6 ACCOUNTABILITY

How do you develop an organization where excellent customer service is practiced daily at all levels? You can spend a lot of energy ensuring that your leadership team is trained and that you have correct policies, but it will be a waste of money if the front-line employees are not motivated and trained to implement the policies designed to satisfy your customers. How many times have you had a problem with an employee where you are doing business only to hear "I just work here. You need to talk to my boss."?

One of the keys to consistent, world-class service is to create systems of accountability so that every member of your team is held to a high standard. You should ask yourself the following question, "If our organization had an employee who was mistreating my customers, how long could this go on before we found out about it?" Look for areas or processes where one person has too much authority without any check and balance.

> Ninety-six percent of unhappy customers never
> complain, and of that percentage,
> 91 percent will never buy from that company again.

Rude or improperly trained employees could be losing business for your company, and you never know it. So, how do you develop an accountability process without employees feeling that "big brother" is watching over their shoulders?

Leaders need to hold their staff accountable. Most employees want to do a good job; unfortunately, most leaders do not provide balanced, timely feedback to help them along the way. An effective leader is always looking for opportunities to coach and develop their staff. This is done using a variety of tools.

- ❖ **Informal feedback.** Look for examples of good and incorrect behaviors to discuss with each employee. Just remember that constructive feedback should be given in private.

- ❖ **Formal Reviews.** The key is simplicity! Each review should contain the following three elements:

  1. Positive Feedback. What did the employee do that was excellent or above your expectations?

  2. Constructive Feedback. What should the employee start doing, stop doing or improve?

  3. Job-Specific Goals. Develop, in advance, four or five measurable goals and record whether the employee met, partially met, or did not meet the goals.

  *How frequently should you conduct reviews?* This depends on how long an employee has been with your organization.

During the first year, it is important to provide regular feedback to a new employee to correct bad habits while they can still be changed. A quarterly review would usually provide the feedback in a timely manner.

For everyone else, performance reviews should be given twice a year. Quarterly reviews leave the leadership feeling like they are always in the middle of writing and delivering reviews. Annual reviews, which most organizations adopt, allow too much time in between formal feedback. This is especially true for the majority of organizations where the only balanced feedback they receive is during a formal review.

***Balanced Reviews.*** Many people, especially those new to leadership positions, are afraid to deliver constructive feedback during a review. Several years ago, I was working with a client and ran into a situation with a particular employee. The customer surveys we had conducted painted a picture of this employee providing extremely poor service and inexcusable conduct when dealing with a group of customers. When discussing this situation with the leadership team, I heard statements such as: "I'm not surprised. That has been going on for years."

Following the meeting, I went to visit the Human Resources Department and asked to review this employee's personnel file. What do you think I found in the past three years worth of reviews? Nothing but glowing comments! You would have thought this person was a model employee.

In my years of working with companies and performing assessments for businesses, I have yet to meet a "perfect" person. Everyone has some skill or behavior that could be improved. The point of a review is to provide both the positive and constructive feedback so the employee can make improvements. A review without something to work on does not do the employee any long-term favors.

As I look back over my career, I am thankful to the one or two supervisors who had the courage to tell me that I needed to improve in a particular area. I may not have been happy at the time, and most always disagreed with their assessment, but looking back, I am grateful they gave me the opportunity to improve.

❖ **Employee Recognition Programs.** Utilize a system appropriate for the area to encourage team and individual behaviors that benefit the customers. Celebrate the victories, especially if you receive positive feedback from a customer!

Don't be afraid to deal with poor performers and inappropriate behaviors. Many leaders feel that having a warm body in a role is better than having a vacant position. This is simply not correct! Failing to deal with poor performance drags the rest of the team down and lowers standards. Top-performing employees appreciate it when their leader deals with personnel problems. Give the opportunity for an employee to respond to your feedback, but don't hesitate to terminate someone if it is not working out.

> **Failing to deal with poor performance drags the rest of the team down and lowers standards.**

Finally, ensure that your leadership team is not isolated in an executive suite. Get out and spend time with your staff and customers. I recommend every leader spending several hours every two weeks interacting with their customers and soliciting their feedback. Executives have a tendency to get caught up in their management responsibilities. They forget that their primary responsibility is to develop their team and remove roadblocks so that the front-line employees can meet the needs of your customers.

Accountability systems will help ensure that your policies are executed and your customers are treated just as you would treat them if you could be in multiple places at once.

# CULTURE CORNERSTONES

## WHAT?

❑ *Create a culture of accountability.*

## HOW?

❑ *Provide regular, balanced feedback to all employees every six months.*

❑ *Ensure leadership gets out of their office and observes the work of their team.*

## BENEFIT?

❑ *Employees will recognize that their actions, even when not being watched, must meet the standards of the organization.*

❑ *Personal growth will take place in each individual, resulting in a more skilled work force.*

# 7 | GUEST RECOVERY

**M**any organizations can perform well and look good when things are going well, but you can tell a lot about the quality of an organization when you see how they respond when there are problems. Do you work for a perfect organization that never makes a mistake? If so, you can skip to Chapter 8. For those of you who are honest, continue reading this chapter on Guest Recovery.

Whether you call the people you serve guests, clients or customers, the following principles apply. All organizations are going to make mistakes, even if it is only in the perception of your customers. Great organizations see these momentary failures as opportunities to prove to a client that you do value their business. During my customer-service workshops, I often divide the attendees into groups of three and ask them to share amongst themselves a good and bad customer service experience that they have encountered as a consumer.

In almost every group, there are examples of how a situation started out as a bad experience, but due to the response and action of an employee or manager, it turned out to be the example of excellent service that they remember.

Let me give a few examples of guest recovery that have been shared in some of these sessions.

# A Near Barbecue Botch!

A woman in a recent class, I'll call her Paige, shared the following story about a Christmas present she almost didn't get. She had gone to one of the home improvement stores and selected a barbecue grill that was going to be the main Christmas present for her husband. She selected a particular brand and model and found out that the only one remaining was the floor sample. This worked for her as it was already assembled.

Wanting to make this a surprise, she made arrangements to pay for the grill and pick it up several weeks later on Christmas Eve. Paige confirmed with the employee that they would put her grill in the back and mark it as sold. He reassured her that it would be waiting for her on Christmas Eve.

Running around in a mad, last-minute shopping scramble, Paige made an early stop by the home improvement store to pick up the grill. After the employee spent several minutes hunting in the back room, he returned to inform her that it was no longer there. Apparently, another employee had sold the grill, even though it was clearly marked as being taken. Paige was upset!

Paige then explained how the very bad situation made a quick turnaround. The employee immediately apologized for the mistake and alerted the store manager. He also apologized and started working on a solution. He told Paige that they would do whatever they needed to make her happy. He asked her to select another grill that was similar in features to the one she had purchased. She chose one that happened to be the next model up from the one previously purchased. It was almost $100 more, but the manager said that would be fine.

The manager checked the computer to see if they had a new one in stock as the floor model had a dent on the cover.

Unfortunately, their store was out of that particular grill. He checked their other stores and found one remaining grill across town.

As most of us are on Christmas Eve, Paige was on a tight time schedule. The manager took down her address and assured her that they would deliver the grill that afternoon.

True to his word, the manager showed up with the grill assembled with a large bow on the top. He again apologized for the mix-up and gave Paige a small gift certificate to their store.

This was an example of how the actions of a store manager turned a very bad situation into a positive one. Let's look at an example of a missed opportunity:

# Dry Cleaning

One of the first things that I always attempt to do when moving into a new neighborhood is find a dependable dry cleaner. I want a good rate, but more importantly, I want my clothes to be clean, stain free, and without broken buttons.

We settled on a dry cleaner close to our home and began using them on a weekly basis. Things went fine for almost a year. I would drive by, drop off my bag and then pick it up after 5:00 p.m. the same day.

When hanging up my clothes one day after making a pickup from the cleaners, I noticed that one of the pairs of pants did not belong to me. I returned the pants the next day, hoping that the rightful owner would be located. The owner of the establishment did not even offer a word of thanks for bringing back the pants.

One day, I went to pick up a load of shirts as I prepared for a week on the road. Four of my favorite shirts were missing from my order at the cleaners. The owner of the establishment insisted that someone must have picked them up earlier. I called my wife and verified that this was not the case.

The owner acted frustrated when I told him that they had been misplaced and that I really needed them by the close of business the following day. He did not apologize, but said in a harsh tone, "Give me some time. I will find them and give you a call."

By the following afternoon, I had not heard from the cleaners, so I stopped by and went inside. The owner had forgotten that he was supposed to be looking for my shirts. I again reminded him of the situation, and he asked if I could attempt to spot them as he forwarded the carousel of finished clothes.

Sure enough. The third or fourth items to go by were my shirts. They had been tagged for a different customer. (Who knows if I would have ever seen them if I had not found them first!)

The owner handed me my clothes and did not offer any explanation or even a simple, "I'm sorry about that." What he did do was make sure he got the $5.00 bill posted to my account prior to my leaving the cleaners.

The very next week, several shirts that belonged to some poor soul were combined with mine. Once again, I returned the shirts. This time I asked if he was having trouble with his help. This had been the third mistake in three weeks.

No response.

That was the last time I visited that particular cleaners.

Fortunately, there are dry cleaners on all four corners of the intersection near my home. I selected a new one that had just opened. So far, so good.

These two examples demonstrate the importance of proper recovery when a mistake is made. Let's compare and contrast these two stories.

In the first example, the customer was very upset to learn that the gift she purchased for her husband was gone. If the manager had not stepped in when he did, Paige would have probably not stopped with the store manager. She would have voiced her dissatisfaction up the chain of command within that particular company. It would have most likely been the last time she set foot in that store, and she would have told all her friends about the bad experience.

There were several important aspects to the recovery of the barbecue grill.

1. The employee who first discovered the problem immediately took responsibility for the mistake and apologized to the customer.

2. The front-line employee then involved management to help solve the problem.

3. The manager also apologized and then immediately began working on an acceptable solution.

4. The manager offered an alternative of greater value and confirmed with his customer that this would be satisfactory.

5. The manager took personal responsibility to resolve the problem.

6. In addition to providing the replacement grill, the manager offered to deliver it to the customer's home.

7. The manager added a nice extra touch by putting a large bow on the grill when it was delivered.

8. The customer received a gift certificate that provided an incentive for her to return to the store and give them the opportunity to prove that this was an isolated experience.

The above steps show how to handle a recovery situation. We can also learn from negative examples. In the "Dry Cleaning" example, there were several mistakes made in the way they responded to the situation:

1. When confronted with each mistake, the owner failed to offer a simple apology.

2. After the misplaced shirts and two days to find them, the proper thing to do would have been to apologize and give them to me at no charge.

3. When dealing with several of the issues, the owner showed frustration toward me, his customer.

4. The end result was his loss of my business and a gain for his competitor across the street.

So, how do you prepare for mistakes that are unpredictable and can vary from day to day and customer to customer? The key is common sense. Ask yourself, "How would I want to be treated if that were to happen to me?"

Another key point is to train your staff and leadership to view problems as opportunities to create a loyal customer, instead of annoyances. For several years, I had the privilege of managing an internal call center for Walt Disney World. This group received calls from other Disney "Cast Members" when they had a problem with their computers or software programs.

When talking with the group, I would frequently ask: "How many times did you receive a call from a customer telling you that everything was perfect with their system today?" The question received a laugh as they all realized that their role was to deal with problems and offer solutions. Customers never called them to let them know everything was fine. In many cases, the person on the other end of the phone was upset and irritated that they had to deal with the problem instead of spending time on their own tasks.

My challenge to each of the call center employees was to have a goal of ending the conversation with the customer thanking them for their assistance with their problem being resolved. There are several steps required to take an angry customer on the other end of the phone to the point where you end with a polite exchange of words and mutual respect.

## 1. Listen

❖ Listen carefully without interrupting the customer. Interrupting appears defensive and tends to add "fuel to the fire."

❖ Get into listening position, stop what you are doing and give your full attention … remember, this is your opportunity to turn a dissatisfied customer into a loyal and satisfied customer.

❖ Give customers a chance to share their concerns, frustrations and feelings.

## 2. Empathize & Apologize

❖ For example, in the case of our system support center, saying something like, *"I understand how frustrating it can be when you are up against a deadline and can't meet it due to a system issue."*

❖ Acknowledge the customer's concerns or problem, *"I am really sorry that you had this experience … I can see how this could be very frustrating for you."*

❖ A simple "I'm sorry" can go a long way toward reducing the anger and frustration the customer is feeling. *Until a customer hears those words, he or she may not be ready to move forward to resolve the problem.*

❖ If you are dealing with the situation in person, nod your head to demonstrate that you are hearing what they are saying.

❖ Express sincere concern … you understand the impact on the customer and their business/department.

## 3. Don't Justify

❖ The customer wants a cure, NOT excuses or who's to blame.

❖ The customer isn't concerned with your problems at this point.

❖ It looks bad for your organization, no matter which area or areas are at fault!

❖ **YOU** are the company to the customer.

## 4. Ask Questions

❖ For example, *"What specifically happened when the system went down? We want to make sure we solve the right problem."*

❖ You want to respond quickly, but you also want to make sure you understand the problem in order to offer the appropriate solution.

❖ You may need to understand specific information.

❖ Confirm that you have an accurate understanding of the "REAL" problem.

❖ By asking questions and sincerely listening, you have involved the customer in solving the problem.

## 5. Agree to a Course of Action

❖ For example, *"We can do a couple of things to help you meet your commitments and correct the problem … do these work for you?"*

❖ Provide some possible solutions to address the concerns. Confirm that the solutions will meet your customer's needs and expectations.

❖ <u>WARNING:</u> COMMITTING TO AN ACTION THAT YOU OR YOUR ORGANIZATION/DEPARTMENT CANNOT FOLLOW THROUGH ON MAY BE HARMFUL TO THE RELATIONSHIP.

❖ Make sure that when you commit to an action/solution that you involve the proper people/departments, especially if you are counting on their support or action to follow through to satisfy the customer.

## 6. Check to Make Sure Action Is Completed

❖ For example, *"I just wanted to make sure that the actions we took met your needs. Is there anything else we can do to help?"*

❖ Call, e-mail or make an appointment with your customer asking if they were completely satisfied with the action taken to resolve the problem. Did you address the issue that caused the dissatisfaction?

In summary, mistakes are going to happen. It is not the mistake itself that defines an organization but how they respond and recover that determines if you will keep your customer and even improve the relationship you have with them.

# CULTURE CORNERSTONES

## WHAT?

☐ Create a culture that tries to minimize errors but views mistakes as a normal part of doing business and an opportunity to learn and get better at what you do.

☐ When handled properly, a service problem can become an opportunity to transform an average customer into a loyal fan.

## HOW?

☐ Train leadership to view problems as a teaching opportunity, not as the time to get after an employee.

☐ Establish practices for dealing with the most common types of problems and customer complaints.

☐ Train every employee on how to diffuse an upset customer.

## BENEFIT?

☐ Once skilled at dealing with difficult situations, employees will look at a problem as an opportunity, rather than an annoyance. This will increase their job satisfaction and reduce the stress associated with their job.

☐ If a proper recovery occurs, the customer can become a vocal advocate for your products or services, resulting in additional business.

☐ If mistakes are handled politely and promptly, the chance of a more costly remedy, including legal action against your organization, will decrease.

# 8 | RESPONSIVENESS – A CULTURE OF SPEED

**A** Quick Response! This is one of the best-kept secrets to success. It does not matter if you are in a sales role dealing with a potential client or responding to a problem with a customer. The quicker you handle the situation, the better chance you have of it turning out the way you desire.

Let's talk about how this applies in the world of sales. Several years ago, I had the opportunity to perform a mystery shopper, competitive comparison engagement for one of my clients. I set up meetings with five companies who provided services in the area of interest.

One company clearly stood out from the other four. Not only were they the most organized in their presentation, but they were the first one to get back to me with answers to my questions. They were polite and regularly called to check on the status of my purchasing decision. I never heard from three of the remaining four, and one company took over a week to respond to my questions.

There is a fine line to walk when dealing with the sales process. You want to be responsive to the client, but not annoy them with excessive communication. This company understood that balance. They had a culture of speed! The company was so impressive that my client ended up joining forces with them at a later date.

## A Long Wait

Our society is growing more impatient every year. The expectation has been set that we can have what we want and get it when we want it. This may be a result of improved technology and an increased dependence on fast-food restaurants. We are also getting busier. We fill our days with constant activities. No one can relate to this more than parents of teenagers who spend hours shuttling their children to an endless list of activities.

The number one turnoff for the average customer is a long wait. We expect to be served. As part of my regular travels, I often have the need to rent a vehicle. On one trip, I arrived in Orlando at 10:30 p.m. and picked up my luggage. I proceeded to the rental car counter, only to find a line that snaked back and forth four times through their dividers.

Being interested in how organizations respond to situations like this, I waited in line for ten minutes and timed the rate of service. Counting the number of customers in front of me, I determined that it would be over an hour before it would be my turn. They were operating three out of twelve stations. Most of their rentals are by reservation, so you have to wonder about the person who did their scheduling! (But that's a different story.)

I politely approached the counter, in between customers and asked the employee if there was any way they could get some additional help to speed up this process. She pointed me to the gentleman at the end of the counter who was their manager on duty. I again waited until he had finished with his current customer, and then asked him if there was any chance they could call some additional help.

He looked up from his computer and made the following statement: "If you don't like the wait, go somewhere else." (Yes, he actually said those words!) Apparently, he was there to collect his paycheck and really did not care about the level of service provided to his customers.

A critical step toward becoming an excellent customer service organization is creating a culture of speed! This does not mean that everyone is always running around in a panic, but when *any* employee in your organization sees a long line or a delay in providing your product or service, they should kick into high gear.

Many of you may be saying, "That's fine for most people, but my job has natural spurts of high activity. I would be out of business if I staffed to handle the peak times."

That is true, but there is still something you can do to address the long wait issue. It has to do with attitude. As I mentioned earlier, during my time with Walt Disney World, I had the privilege of managing an internal call center for system problems. When I inherited the group, we had an average hold time of around 15 minutes. (Yes, people actually waiting on the phone that long to talk to a technician. It made it a bit more tolerable that we had entertaining Disney soundtracks playing as the hold music.)

During my first few days, I noticed that even when there were 20 people waiting on hold and the longest wait time was over 20 minutes, the Cast Members and contractors staffing the call center did not seem to be bothered. They would take a few minutes between calls to chat with their friends or get up for one of their scheduled breaks. **There was no sense of urgency!**

We spent the next several weeks changing the culture. The first step was to make it very clear to everyone involved that the length of hold time was unacceptable and was going to be fixed. We collected some data to help us determine the busiest times for customer calls. The graphs clearly showed a trend of a busy period between 9:30 a.m. and 11:00 a.m. and another increase in calls after people returned from lunch around 1:30 p.m.

We also looked at the call data and determined that Tuesday was consistently the busiest day of the week. Why Tuesday? That was my question for the staff. No one really knew the answer. It was only after some digging that I determined that the Information Technology department rolled out all software changes on Monday night!

Armed with these two pieces of information, we went to work adjusting our behaviors to solve the hold-time problem. The first change was to shift all breaks so we had all hands on deck during our two peak periods. Secondly, we went to a four-day, ten hour-per-day work week and all staff worked on Tuesday, our busiest day.

The last change helped to raise the level of attention to the long hold times. We installed a display board that would beep any time someone was on hold longer than our acceptable length of time. Everyone hated that buzzer, but when it went off, everyone jumped on a phone and worked to bring the hold times back within the acceptable range!

We made some other changes in the way the group was organized. Without increasing our budget, we were able to decrease hold times so that many calls were answered on the first ring, or at worst, hold times were two minutes.

## Unavoidable Waits

There may be times in your business where there are peaks of activity and some lines are unavoidable. There are two key ways to minimize the negative impact on your customer:

1. Acknowledge the wait time and apologize to the customer for the inconvenience.

2. Show some urgency! The customer will tolerate a wait if they feel you are doing everything possible to provide your product or service as fast as you can.

### *Valet Parking*

To illustrate the second point above, let's look at an example from the valet parking industry. There are times when an event concludes and the valet service is flooded with customers. Yes, they should be staffed at a level to handle the customers, but some lines are unavoidable.

The customers waiting in line will be watching the valet staff. People may not want to wait to get their car, but if they see the parking attendants hustling from one car to the next, they will tend to relax and cut the valet company some slack. On the other hand, if waiting customers observe the employees talking amongst themselves or walking to retrieve their vehicles, they will become more irritated with the long wait. Again, the key principle is to demonstrate a true sense of urgency when serving your customers.

## Get Me Off That Plane!

One of the good and bad aspects of my job is that I frequently find myself on a plane heading to visit one of my clients. As with anyone who travels frequently, the less time you have to spend on the plane the better. After a flight of any length, the last thing you want to do is pull up at the gate and have to wait while the ground crew gets prepared to let you off the plane.

Southwest Airlines understands this point! I make regular trips between Dallas and Houston utilizing Southwest Airlines. I noticed a difference with this airline, compared to some of the other major carriers. Very rarely do I wait more than two minutes after the fasten seatbelt light goes off and I see people ahead of me moving toward the exit. This doesn't happen by chance.

During my last trip back to Dallas, I watched out the window as my plane approached the gate. There was a small army of ground employees waiting for the plane to reach a final stop. There were luggage handlers with their equipment ready to transport our bags to the baggage claim area. There was someone at the end of the jetway ready to move it up next to the plane. The flight attendants were ready the moment the Jetway was in place and opened the door for their customers to deplane.

It takes several groups working together to make this a great experience. They have developed a culture of speed! They understand that their customers are ready to get off the plane and on to their business or back to their families.

Contrast that with some other experiences where my plane arrived at the gate, only to have to wait five to 10 minutes before the door was opened. The captain came on the intercom to inform us that we had "snuck up on the gate crew," and they were not ready for us. (This is difficult to believe as they know where every plane is anywhere in the sky!) Any goodwill they had earned by getting us to our destination ahead of schedule was lost! Looking out the window, I noticed ground employees casually walking to their positions, obviously in no hurry.

## Responding to Customer Feedback

There is another aspect of running an organization where a culture of speed is critical. It is in how quickly you respond to customer feedback. When you receive feedback, either through your surveys or completely unsolicited, you have a narrow window of opportunity to respond, resulting in a positive experience for your customers.

Take a look at the following chart:

# Client Feedback/ Response Impact

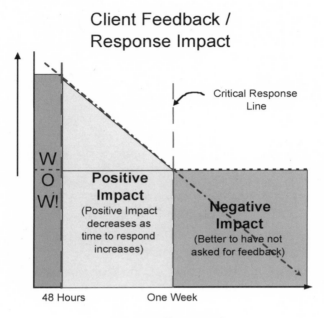

### Client Feedback / Response Impact

Critical Response Line

W
O
W!

**Positive Impact**
(Positive Impact decreases as time to respond increases)

**Negative Impact**
(Better to have not asked for feedback)

48 Hours          One Week

Time to Respond

Depending on the industry and the expectations of your customers, you have approximately 48 hours from the time you receive the feedback to the time you respond to create a "WOW" experience. You will then have the remaining portion of a week to have some positive impact with your customers if you can reply in that window. Following that initial week after feedback, the impact begins to be one of a negative nature.

Let's look at a couple of examples to illustrate this point. First on the positive side:

## Missing Report

Imagine the following scenario: You are a manager in a large company, and you are responsible for several departments. To manage one of these areas, you have grown accustomed to a monthly activity report that comes from one of your vendors. This report helps you identify any potential problem, and you use the numbers in the departmental summary report to give your boss an update.

For some reason, this report does not arrive one month as it has for years. You assume it must just be late and figure out a way to work around not having it. This continues for several months. You are very busy and can't find the right person at this vendor company to call to see why the report has ceased.

You receive a call from someone conducting a customer satisfaction survey on behalf of that vendor. During your feedback, you mention that you really would like to start receiving that helpful report again. You end the call and think, "I doubt anything will come from that."

Two hours later, you receive a call from the account manager from the vendor company. He quickly apologizes for the inconvenience caused by the interruption in the delivery of this report. He lets you know that the report will start arriving again on Thursday and offers to print and deliver the back reports that were missing.

What would your response be if you were that customer? If you are like me, after you pick yourself up from the floor, you are probably pretty impressed that someone would respond the same day and actually have a solution to the problem. You are also more likely to continue doing business with that company. That is the power of a culture of speed. The process was in place to enable quick exchange of information, resulting in a customer need being met and their expectation exceeded. This is what I refer to as a "WOW" experience.

Now, let's examine what can happen if you end up on the right-hand side of the chart and a slow response ends up hurting your organization.

## Grand Opening

It was GRAND OPENING day! For months, we had watched the construction and anticipated the opening of a new grocery store in our neighborhood. (It may sound strange to be excited about a new grocery store, but our only other local option was sorely lacking in quality and customer service.)

There were balloons in the parking lot. Extra management had been brought in for the occasion. Every employee was on their best behavior, demonstrating manners that would have made their grandma proud!

There were free samples on every aisle and every checkout lane was open and ready to take your money.

As we walked up and down every aisle, trying to figure out the layout of this new store, my wife noticed that they did not carry several items that she commonly purchases.

Just about that time, one of the managers walked by and asked us if he could help us in any way. We mentioned the items that were missing from the shelves. The manager asked for our name and number and wrote the information about the items on the back of my business card. He said, "I will check into this and get back to you soon."

That was six months ago and we have yet to hear from the store. During the first two or three days, I would have been impressed to have received a call from the manager, even if the response was that they could not obtain our requested items. If the call had come anytime in the week following our visit, I would have still been favorably impressed.

After the second week, they crossed into that right-hand side of the chart. The entire experience turned negative! We rarely stop at that particular store and even travel several miles down the road to shop at a grocery store that understands the importance of customer service.

Creating a culture of responsiveness can be tiring, but it is a critical part of the fabric of any successful organization.

# CULTURE CORNERSTONES

## WHAT?

☐ Create a culture of speed in the following areas:
- *Responding to customer feedback*
- *Delivering your products or services*

## HOW?

☐ *Leadership should demonstrate a sense of urgency when responding to customer problems.*

☐ *Encourage employees to view what they do through the eyes of a customer. Instead of entering a doctor's office through the back door when returning from lunch, walk through the waiting room to see the volume of people seated there.*

☐ *Create measurements that track the time to respond to customers or changes in your business. For example, if you work in a call center, diligently track the time a customer spends on hold.*

## BENEFIT?

☐ *We are an impatient society. Customers will find an alternative if they are forced to wait.*

☐ *Customers will tolerate wait times if they think the employees are doing everything possible to provide the service in a timely manner.*

# 9 TEAMWORK

**W**ouldn't life be easier if we didn't have to deal with people? Unless you are a small, one-person organization, delivering excellent customer service requires working with other co-workers, vendors and partners. You can work as hard as you like and personally do a great job in your area, but unless everyone else on your team delivers on their piece of the pie, great service will not happen.

Creating a culture of teamwork does not happen by accident! It requires hard work and strong interpersonal skills of all team members to come together and provide an excellent product or service for your customers. This chapter covers seven key elements of teamwork that are essential for your organization if you are serious about becoming known for your customer service.

## Recognize Common Goals and Objectives

The first thing that any team must have in order to look and act like a winning organization is to have a set of common goals and objectives. The reason most people think of sports organizations when they think about a team is because they have a built-in goal and objective:

Win as many contests as possible! This allows them to come together and focus their energy on a common goal.

Ken Blanchard's book, *One Minute Manager*, explains that not having goals for an organization is like trying to bowl without seeing the pins. Picture yourself rolling your first ball. A split second before striking the pins, a curtain falls between you and the pins. You hear the ball crash into the pins and can tell some have been knocked down.

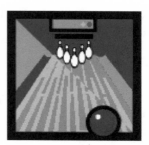

Now you are ready to throw the second ball. The curtain is still down. How do you decide where to aim the ball? (If you are like me, it is probably all luck if you hit any pins, but you get the point.)

That is how people in your organization will feel if there is not a well-defined set of goals.

The simple picture to the right is an illustration of teamwork, and it reminds me of a quote that I like:

### *"It is hard to rock the boat when you are busy rowing."*

There is a lot of truth to that statement when you stop and think about the concept. When your team is busy accomplishing an objective, they tend to stay focused on the work. They do not have the time to cause problems or disrupt the unity within your organization.

## Utilize the Entire Team

Every person on a team, including the leader, has a role to play. The sooner everyone grasps this concept and realizes that no one is better or more important than another, the more effective your team will become. Often leaders feel that because of their position of authority within the organization, they are smarter or more talented than those they supervise. Leaders are in a unique position with their own responsibilities. They can only be successful if the rest of the team delivers on their roles.

Effective teams know how to use the leader and his/her position of authority when it comes to delivering great customer service. At a restaurant my family enjoys frequenting, they understand this concept. If *anything* goes wrong with the guest experience, all the servers, hosts/hostesses and other staff have been trained to notify the manager on duty.

The manager then has the ability to interact with the guest and attempt to recover appropriately. For this to work, the staff must feel comfortable bringing problems to the attention of their manager, realizing that the ultimate goal is to do what is right for the customer.

It is a funny phenomenon in our society, but people tend to give more respect to those in authority. How many times have you asked, "Can I speak to your manager?" A customer could be very upset with a particular employee, but when they have the opportunity to discuss the situation with a supervisor or manager, they usually calm down. (This is assuming that the manager knows how to communicate with an upset customer.)

This same principle is true for various groups within your team. Several years ago, I worked with a client who was experiencing challenges in the area of teamwork. The department was divided into four teams. Every morning, the teams received the cases that they were responsible for investigating and resolving. One day, Team A received some cases that ended up not requiring a lot of follow up or intense investigation. That same day, Team B received very difficult cases, requiring a lot of interaction with the media.

What we found was that Team A on this day finished their work by mid-afternoon. Team B worked well into the evening. The members of Team A relaxed and took advantage of being done early, while their co-workers struggled just down the hall. We had to change the culture!

After several discussions and other events, we convinced all members of the department that they needed to be more concerned about the members on the other teams. It was not possible for someone finishing early to take over a case for the other team, but they could lend a hand returning a call or even filing information in the proper place.

When you develop a culture where all employees are looking for ways to assist their co-workers, it becomes an exciting place to work, and the end customer is the ultimate winner!

## Don't blame or point the finger

One of the quickest ways to tear down teamwork is to have one member of the team blame or "point the finger" in the direction of another team member.

The longer I live, the more I have learned the importance of getting both sides of a story before drawing a conclusion. Part of building a successful team requires creating a culture where every employee develops the practice of gathering the facts and looking at the big picture before pointing a finger of blame.

This does not mean that you look the other way and ignore a problem. The key is to always focus on how the individuals and organization can learn from a negative experience and avoid repeating it.

One way to remove some of the emotion and focus on the facts is to use the following model when analyzing a mistake. Follow a problem or service delivery error, and once the customer is satisfied, calmly discuss these questions:

- ❖ What was supposed to happen?
- ❖ What actually happened?
- ❖ What accounts for any difference?
- ❖ How was the problem corrected?
- ❖ What can be learned?

It is unavoidable to name the individuals involved in a problem, but the focus should be on learning from the mistake, and not on punishing the individuals involved. Once everyone adopts that attitude, there will be a lot less finger pointing and negative discussion and more of a continuous improvement culture.

## Be Understanding

This picture of an iceberg is a great reminder of the next secret to developing great teamwork. Develop a culture of compassion and understanding!

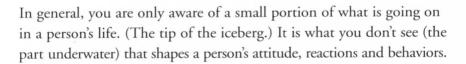

When you look at this picture, what jumps out at you? For me, it is the fact that the visible part of the iceberg is only a small fraction of the total. This is how you should view people, customers, co-workers, leaders and employees.

In general, you are only aware of a small portion of what is going on in a person's life. (The tip of the iceberg.) It is what you don't see (the part underwater) that shapes a person's attitude, reactions and behaviors.

In working with clients in the area of dealing with angry customers, I often hear the comment:

### *"I can't believe they got so bent out of shape over such a small thing."*

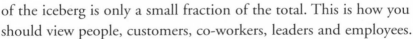

73

What this person does not realize is that the "small thing" may have just been the item that sent someone over the edge. Faced with that issue on its own, the customer or co-worker may not have reacted the same way.

Both at work and at home, it is good to allow people a little space. This also applies to the relationship between a leader and his/her employees. On the vast majority of days, your leader may appear to be a happy, balanced individual. One particular morning, you walk into his/her office to discuss an issue and receive a verbal lashing for several non-related items.

In a culture of understanding, you know not to judge that individual solely from one experience. You never know what is going on "under the water." That leader could have just received bad news from a doctor or experienced the loss of a friend. You never know what triggered the response that was out of the ordinary. (However, this does not excuse profane or abusive language or behavior.)

## Share the Burden

It is rare to find someone who will admit that they don't have enough to keep them busy. Unless you were the job applicant who was told, "We don't have enough work to keep you busy." He replied, "Oh, you would be amazed at how little it takes!"

Most of us long for more hours in the day to accomplish all that is on our plate. The truth is that everyone has days that are busier than others. The key to this element of teamwork culture is to train everyone to constantly look for ways to help out others on the team. It may be as simple as offering to return a file or proof a document. Even these small gestures, if done without the expectation of a payback, will create an atmosphere of teamwork.

If you have had the rare pleasure to work as part of a team that functions at this level, it is an exciting place to be. This also applies to those in leadership positions. Their roles are not to perform the tasks assigned to their employees, but they should be ready and willing to lend a hand when someone is overwhelmed with work.

## Share the Credit

You and your small team of co-workers have been working for several months on a very important project. You sacrifice many weekends and evenings in order to meet the aggressive deadline. The project is completed on time and under budget and is a huge success for your company.

You learn that your boss is given the opportunity to present an overview of the project to the executive team and is also given a promotion with a nice raise. Meanwhile, the rest of the employees on the team did not even receive as much as a thank you from the leadership of the company. How would you feel?

If you are like most people, you would think twice before giving up your personal time in the future to work on a project for your boss.

Now, compare that with how you would feel if the leader had chosen to share the credit with the team. Instead of grabbing the glory, your leader could have invited the team to help out with the presentation at the executive team meeting. Each team member could have taken a section of the presentation. Not only would each have gained from the experience of presenting to their executive committee, they would probably be the ones who were the most knowledgeable about the details of the project.

The previous leader missed an opportunity to unite the team like few things can do. One of the basic needs of any employee or volunteer is to feel that their work has been appreciated. Organizations need to start measuring the effectiveness of a leader, not based on what they personally do, but on the success of the team they lead.

This not only applies to those in leadership positions, but it is also equally important for each employee to grasp, regardless of the position or title. Humility is not a personality attribute in large supply in our society. It is rare, and very refreshing, to work with someone who is quick to share praise with others who have been involved in the success.

## One Face to the Customer

How many times have you been dealing with a problem, only to be told by an employee "I'm sorry, but I don't work in that department." A customer does not want to, nor should they have to, understand your organizational chart in order to do business with your company. Being given the runaround from one department to another is one of the top customer turnoffs.

Each employee must understand that THEY represent the entire company to the individual with whom they are speaking. This is called the "One Face" principle.

During my time with Walt Disney World, I learned that this was a principle that was trained and practiced. On many occasions, I would take my lunch hour and walk through one of the theme parks. (There is nothing like riding the train around Magic Kingdom and seeing the joy on the faces of children and adults to help you get over a tough day at the office.)

Unfortunately, I was dressed in a shirt and tie and stood out from the thousands of tourists in more comfortable attire. It was very common to be walking through the park and have a guest stop me and ask for directions. As a "Cast Member," I then had the responsibility to either take them to where they were going or introduce them to someone who could. It was not an option to say, "I'm sorry. I work in the

Information Technology Department. I don't have anything to do with operating this park."

Understanding that each employee, from the receptionist to the president, is a representative of their organization is the key.

Building a culture of teamwork is as difficult as the diversity of the people who make up a team. It is not an easy task, but the concepts discussed in this chapter will start you down the right road.

# CULTURE CORNERSTONES

## WHAT?

☐ *Create a culture of teamwork.*

## HOW?

☐ *Proactively encourage team activities, such as cross-functional groups formed to address a particular issue.*

☐ *Do not become so rigid in your job descriptions that an employee is unwilling to jump in and help serve a customer.*

☐ *Develop and train on the "team concept of service" within your organization.*

## BENEFIT?

☐ *A well-functioning team is more effective at serving the customer than individuals all looking out for their own interests.*

☐ *It is fun to work on a successful team! Turnover will decrease and employee morale will increase when co-workers learn to value each other's contribution.*

| 10 | # GOOD, BETTER, BEST! |
|---|---|

**M**any people go through life doing just enough to get by. Companies that create a culture of excellent customer service have figured out how to get more from their leaders, employees and volunteers.

My wife, Heather, has always used a teaching model with our children. In order to help them make good decisions, she talks to them about good, better and best. For example, when my son, Tony, meets an adult for the first time, the following is how Heather prepares him for the moment:

**Good** would be if Tony shook the person's hand and said "hello."

**Better** would be if Tony shook the person's hand, made eye contact, told them his name and said it was nice to meet them.

**Best** would be if Tony did all of the above and then engaged the adult in some simple conversation, such as asking them how their day had been so far.

Many parents would be thrilled to get a consistent "Good" level of behavior from their children. We attempt to use every opportunity as a teaching moment to train our children to not be content with the minimum standard, but to strive for the best in everything they do.

I was recently on a business/vacation trip to Orlando. Another close friend and client was also there with his family. I stopped by to see them one afternoon. He told me the story of their arrival at the Orlando airport the night before. It immediately made me think of the Good, Better, Best principle.

## Exceptional Luggage Assistance

It was late on Sunday evening and my friend, David, and his wife and five children ages 3 to 14 arrived at the Orlando airport for a week's stay visiting friends. With a family that large, they came with a lot of luggage!

David and his wife, Becky, were tired from the trip and anxious to reach the home of their former neighbors where they would be staying for the week. They knew that these friends were planning a late dinner after the arrival. The family of seven made their way from the terminal, down the escalator to the baggage claim area.

It was there that they were pleasantly surprised. They were greeted by a luggage handler, Calvin, with his large cart. "Sir, may I help you with your luggage this evening?"

When you have five children, including two little ones, hauling your own luggage is not an option.

"Sure," David responded.

After introducing himself, Calvin asked David if they were planning on renting a car.

"Yes, we are," David responded.

Calvin said, "There have been five very large planes that landed in the last few minutes. Things are going to get crazy down at the rental car counters. If you are comfortable with it, why don't you leave your wife and kids with me. We will wait for your luggage while you go get your rental car."

David took him up on the offer. He beat the crowd and met Calvin and his family just as he finished up the paperwork.

"That worked great!" David said, thanking Calvin.

"I will help you out to your rental car," Calvin added.

They walked past many other families. David noticed that the other skycaps were leaving the luggage on the curb and returning inside to handle a new customer.

Calvin followed David and his family all the way to their rental car. He helped them load the luggage and asked them if they needed any help finding their destination.

David was so impressed with the exceptional service, he stopped to ask Calvin some questions.

"I noticed that you do a lot more than many of the other skycaps. I didn't see anyone else take the customer's luggage all the way to their rental car. Where did you learn how to provide such good service?" David asked.

Calvin replied. "I worked at Walt Disney World for many years from high school on. I guess what they taught me just stuck. I have found that I enjoy my job better when I provide the best service possible and get to know my customers, even if it is just for a few minutes. I like knowing I saved them some time and got them off to a good start on their vacation."

David continued, "When you first approached me about giving us a hand, I pulled out a $10 dollar bill. That is what I would normally pay for help with our bags. I have been so impressed; I am putting that away and giving you $20."

Calvin expressed his appreciation and wished David and his family a safe trip after making sure they knew how to get out of the airport heading toward their destination.

**Good. Better! Best!!** Let's look at how this applies to this story. The majority of the skycaps working that day would have probably provided a "Good" level of service. It would have looked something like this:

### *Good*

The skycap would have greeted David and his family and offered his assistance with their luggage. They may have made some conversation with the family to find out where they were from and their destination.

They would have waited for the bags, and once collected, the skycap would have taken them down to the next level where David would have found a very long line for the rental car.

Not wanting to miss out on the next customer, the skycap would have walked with the rest of the family to the pickup area for the rental cars and left the bags and returned upstairs.

This would have been the minimal level of acceptable service in this situation.

### *Better*

A slightly more experienced skycap would have taken service to a higher level. After greeting the family and finding out David's plans for the trip, he would have suggested that David head down to get the rental car.

After collecting the bags with the rest of the family, the skycap would have met David on the lower level as he completed the paperwork for his rental car. The skycap would then take the bags to the rental car pickup area and wished the family safe travel.

### *Best*

Calvin knew how to provide excellent service! He took the "Better" level of service up a notch and took the bags all the way to the rental car. This required extra time and effort on his part. Calvin also loaded the bags and made sure his customer knew how to get started toward their destination.

In this day of poor customer service, you will be lucky to receive what we call a "Good" level of service. The challenge every employee and every company will face is how to constantly provide the "BEST" level of service. This will so impress and surprise the customer that they will share the experience with others and, most likely, become a repeat customer.

# CULTURE CORNERSTONES

## WHAT?

☐ *Create a culture where you strive for the BEST!*

## HOW?

☐ *Constantly question the status quo and look for ways to improve on your products or services.*

☐ *Shop the competition to observe practices that may be better than those in place within your organization.*

☐ *Develop a process of sharing "best practices" among different teams or divisions in the company.*

## BENEFIT?

☐ *In a super-competitive economy, only the best in each product or service category will prosper.*

☐ *Employees will take pride in the work they perform when they are recognized as being the best at what they do.*

# 11 | FLEXIBILITY AND COMMON SENSE

*"I'm sorry, but that is our policy,
and I don't have the ability to alter it."*

How many times have you heard that response when you are trying to work through a problem with a company? Standard policies and procedures are important and, if administered properly, can improve the quality of service and help keep costs in check.

The problem occurs when the employee enforcing the policy does not apply common sense to the particular situation. Flexibility! A key to developing customers who return! Recently, I had a couple of experiences that are a perfect illustration of this key to excellent customer service.

# A Tale of Two Pizzas

My family and I were looking for an early dinner before returning to our church for Wednesday activities. There is a family-owned pizza restaurant near our house. We had been there before and really enjoyed their pizza. It was early, so we were just about the only patrons there.

My son happens to be a fan of cheese pizza and does not care for all the other toppings, and my wife and I prefer a good greasy pepperoni pizza. We approached the counter to place our order. The cook took his place just behind the counter and started flipping the dough, trying to convince us of their Italian authenticity. Politely, I told the young lady working the register that I wanted one large pizza. I asked if I could have three-fourths of the pizza with pepperoni and one fourth with cheese. (I also tossed in that I was fine paying for an entire one-ingredient pizza.)

She looked at me and said that they could only split the ingredients on a pizza in half. (The cook was listening to the conversation and was anxious to start building our order.) I restated that I really wanted only a couple of the slices to be cheese for my son. I asked, "Can't you just tell the cook to leave off the pepperoni on a couple of slices?"

Her response was, "No. Our system won't allow us to do that and it will confuse the cook."

After some additional unpleasant exchange of comments, we cancelled our order and left the restaurant.

Several weeks later, we were in the same position on a Wednesday night, and my wife was hungry for a good pizza. She had seen another local pizza restaurant called "Sal's," and we decided to give it a try.

We walked in and were greeted by a friendly young man. It was early and we were again the only people in the place. We were escorted to our table and given the menu.

The waiter took our drink order and then the moment of truth happened ...

I asked if it would be possible to get a large pizza with three-fourths pepperoni and one-fourth cheese. (My wife kicked me under the table, not wanting to go through another unpleasant experience.) The waiter smiled and said, "Sure, I don't see why not." (My wife breathed a sigh of relief and smiled at me.)

The experience and pizza were both great, and we have recommended Sal's many times and would choose their pizza whenever we are hungry for that type of food.

What is the difference between these two experiences?

It is their flexibility and willingness to give the customer what they want. Organizations need standards, policies and rules to operate efficiently, but it is critical that all employees utilize some basic common sense when dealing with customer requests. Your goal should be to satisfy 100 percent of the needs for each customer, within reason. Also, don't let your computer system dictate what you can deliver to your customer. Learn to deal with exceptions!

As another example of this point, there is a phrase that appears on the bottom of many menus that drives me crazy! You can probably guess it: *"No Substitutions Please." When I see that, I read "Mr. Reed, we are not interested in truly meeting your need. Please go elsewhere."* (I'm not talking about asking to substitute a skewer of shrimp for some fries, but for a comparably priced item on the menu.)

Contrast that with another line at the bottom of a menu I saw just this week: *"Anything is possible. Please ask."* That demonstrates a true desire to give the customer what they want, and it dramatically increases the chance that they will be a return customer.

This same concept applies to businesses outside of the hospitality industry. Employees should be trained to ask the question: *"How can I satisfy this request?"* instead of simply answering, *"No, we do not do that."* Many new product and service ideas come from organizations that listen to their customers and make every attempt to tailor their offering to a specific need. Chances are, there are other customers who want the same thing but have been conditioned not to ask.

**Giving your customers exactly what they want will eliminate their desire to go to your competitor!**

Flexibility! Giving your customers exactly what they want will eliminate their desire to go to your competitor! Take a few minutes and review your systems and policies and ask yourself, "How would my employees deal with a request that is slightly different than what we are used to hearing?"

# CULTURE CORNERSTONES

## WHAT?

☐ *Create a culture of common sense!*

## HOW?

☐ *Develop a practice of having outsiders review your policies and business practices. This can be done by another department within your company or by an outside consultant. Someone who is not familiar with your history will spot things that do not make sense and ask the "why do you do that?" question.*

☐ *NEVER allow any employee, including leadership, to use the phrase: "We have always done it that way" when being questioned about a policy or procedure.*

## BENEFIT?

☐ *A lot of waste and inefficiencies have been reduced or eliminated by applying common sense to the everyday tasks.*

☐ *Customers will appreciate your ability to adapt your service within reason to meet their needs. This eliminates the reason for them to try your competition.*

# RESPECT THE CUSTOMER

**12**

Respect is one of the toughest things to develop as part of the culture of an organization. Just as customer service applies both to internal and external customers, so does respect. Without this element in your culture, many of the things discussed earlier in this book will merely be superficial and will come and go depending on who is watching.

It is only through creating a culture where co-workers and customers are genuinely respected that excellent customer service will stick. As I was finishing this chapter, I had an experience that illustrated this point:

## Oops! You Weren't Supposed to See That!

This past week a friend of mine, Randy, received an e-mail from a casual business acquaintance. He informed Randy of some upcoming events with his organization. This person had been on Randy's mind lately as he was interested in talking to him about another business opportunity.

The mission of this organization fit very closely with what he wanted to discuss with him. Randy replied to his e-mail and gave a brief explanation of this topic, requesting a response.

Several days later, Randy received a reply e-mail from the individual. This person's assistant reads and filters all of his e-mails. Included in his reply e-mail was a comment that she had made while passing on the original e-mail.

It read, *"Do you want to reply to him at all?"* I'm sure this person did not intend for that to reach Randy's e-mail. Although it does not seem like a very big deal, it did make Randy feel that they did not value his relationship, either personally or professionally.

Not only is it important to show respect for the customer in e-mails and letters, the same is true on the phone.

Several years ago, I was working with a government agency that provides adoption services. As part of my detailed assessment, I spent some time talking with customers and had some of them complete a survey.

In this case, I was meeting in person with this individual as she told me the following story:

## Supposed to be on Hold!

Julie was a foster parent. (I have grown to have a deep respect for these people!) She was attempting to adopt one of the children in her care and was trying to get an update on the status of her case. The workers responsible for this area had made and broken many promises regarding getting back to her with information.

Julie called the department and asked to talk to the caseworker, Linda. This was Julie's third attempt to reach Linda, and she had left several messages over the past two weeks. Another caseworker answered the phone.

The caseworker was pleasant to Julie and said she would try to locate Linda and asked if she could place her on hold. This is where it went downhill!

The caseworker thought she put Julie on hold, but had apparently not hit the correct button. Julie recounted what she heard as the caseworker conversed with Linda.

"It is that ?@*&? lady, Julie, on the phone again," the caseworker said.

"Tell that ?@?*$ I am not in and take a message," Linda replied.

The caseworker got back on the phone and politely said, "I'm sorry, ma'am. Linda is out of the office this afternoon. May I take a message?"

It was obvious that these two caseworkers had zero respect for their client. Even though they never intended for Julie to hear the conversation, their words were very hurtful.

These two illustrations show what can happen if you fail to develop a culture of respect in your organization. This point is just as true in your personal life as it is in business. We should all strive to treat everyone with the highest respect. This is true whether we personally like them or not!

If you are in a habit of respecting others in your words and actions, regardless of whether they are in your presence, you do not have to worry about someone hearing or seeing something that was not intended for them.

This same principle of respect applies to always telling the truth. I remember my parents telling me, "If you always tell the truth, you don't have to strain to remember what you told someone." We have seen examples of this with our politicians in recent years. Simple slips in what they thought was a "friendly" crowd ended up on the evening news.

So, how do you develop a culture of respect? Try following these principles:

1. Always treat others as you would want to be treated.

2. Ask yourself before every e-mail or conversation, "Would I want what I say or write to be on the front page of the local paper?"

3. If you are in a leadership position, model respectful behavior to your employees. Avoid talking negatively about one employee in front of others.

4. Don't tolerate disrespectful behavior in your organization. With one organization I was part of, we had the following policy: "If you are caught being disrespectful to any potential, current or past customer, you will receive one warning. Upon the second incident, you will be terminated." We never had to reach this second stage with any employee.

Creating a culture of respect is the only way an organization will reach the pinnacle of customer service.

# CULTURE CORNERSTONES

## WHAT?

❏ *Create a culture of respect!*

## HOW?

❏ *Lead by example in the way employees and customers are treated.*

❏ *Don't tolerate disrespectful behavior, either within your organization or to your customers.*

❏ *Measure every action or communication by asking the following question, "How would I feel if what I said or did was printed on the front page of the paper for all to see?"*

## BENEFIT?

❏ *Once a culture of respect is in place, you reduce the likelihood of an employee saying or doing something inappropriately.*

❏ *Creating a culture of respect is the ONLY way you will develop long-lasting excellent customer service.*

# 13 | REACHING THE TOP AND HOLDING ON!

Let's assume that you have built a culture that:

- ❖ Makes a big deal out of little things to keep big things from developing

- ❖ Treats your internal co-workers like customers

- ❖ Values all the aspects of training and development

- ❖ Has implemented the four stages in the customer feedback loop

- ❖ Measures the right things and holds all employees accountable for delivering excellent service

- ❖ Knows how and when to recover when a mistake has been made

- ❖ Is quick to respond and demonstrates a sense of urgency

- ❖ Works effectively as a team

- ❖ Does not settle for good or better, but strives for the best

- ❖ Is flexible and applies common sense as appropriate

- ❖ Respects all customers, both internal and those who buy your products or services, even when not present.

Even the best organizations struggle to do all these things all the time and will fail in one aspect or another. So, how do you put all this together and create a culture of service that lasts and is not dependent on any one leader or individual?

The key lies with the customer feedback loop! Measuring the right things and following through on recovery and process or product changes will ensure that many of the rest of these cultural items are healthy.

The great customer service organizations are not perfect, but if you were to look behind the curtain, you would find that they understand and attempt to practice each of these items.

The following is a customer service culture checkup that will help you identify your strengths and opportunities for improvement. Take the test every six months, responding honestly, and then focus on the specific aspects of your culture that received the lowest scores.

# CUSTOMER SERVICE CULTURE ASSESSMENT

**Directions:** For each characteristic, rate the extent to which the statement is true about your own organization, using this scale:

**0 – Not at all**
**1 – To a small extent**
**2 – To a moderate extent**
**3 – To a great extent**

## Section 1: Take Care of the Small Things

_____ 1. We place the appropriate amount of attention on the details of our work.

_____ 2. Leadership understands the details of our work, but does not micromanage.

_____ 3. Problems are dealt with before they become a big deal.

_____ **Subtotal Section 1**

## Section 2: Great Service Starts Within

_____ 4. Departments that provide services to other internal departments practice good customer service.

_____ 5. Internal departments request feedback from their customers.

_____ 6. Phone calls and e-mails from co-workers are answered in a timely manner.

_____ 7. When a crisis occurs that involves external customers, internal departments assist when possible.

_____ **Subtotal Section 2**

## Section 3: Training and Development

_____ 8. My company has an effective orientation program that helped prepare me for my job.

_____ 9. The orientation program was provided prior to being asked to interact with external customers.

_____ 10. My company provides the training necessary for me to remain current in my position.

_____ 11. Customer service training and refresher sessions are provided regularly.

_____ 12. Leadership training is provided to all those in supervisory positions.

_____ 13. My company has an effective mentoring program to help less-experienced employees develop their skills.

_____ 14. Employees at all levels have a good understanding of our products and services.

_____ 15. Employees are cross-trained so they can fill in for each other when necessary.

_____ 16. All employees are ready to assist a customer or find someone who can when approached by a customer.

_____ **Subtotal Section 3**

## Section 4: Employee Empowerment

_____ 17. There is a process in place that allows any employee to submit customer suggestions or ideas for new or improved products or services.

_____ 18. Ideas that are submitted are considered and acted upon when appropriate.

_____ 19. Employees at all levels are appreciated by those in leadership positions.

_____ 20. Even at lower levels of our organization, employees are empowered to use their judgment when quick action is needed to make things right for a customer.

_____ **Subtotal Section 4**

## Section 5: Customer Feedback Loop

_____ 21. We regularly ask customers to give us feedback about our performance.

_____ 22. The amount of time spent gathering data and producing reports is reasonable.

_____ 23. Employees at all levels have access to reports and measurements needed to perform their job.

_____ 24. Feedback is promptly evaluated to identify trends and areas for improvement.

_____ 25. Adjustments are made in products or services based on customer feedback.

_____ 26. Information from customers is used in designing our products and services.

_____ 27. We maintain measurements of key components of our business and use the results to make needed changes to our processes.

_____ **Subtotal Section 5**

## Section 6: Accountability

_____ 28. We have appropriate measurements in place to ensure our products and services are meeting the needs of the customer.

_____ 29. Employees who do not perform to the expectations of the company and positions are coached or disciplined.

_____ 30. There is an appropriate check-and-balance system in place to prevent the abuse of authority by any employee.

_____ 31. Performance reviews are conducted on time.

_____ 32. Performance reviews contain a mixture of positive and constructive feedback.

_____ 33. We encourage employees at all levels to "shop" the competition to compare their strengths and weaknesses.

_____ **Subtotal Section 6**

## Section 7: Guest Recovery

_____ 34. Employees at all levels understand the importance of recognizing and recovering from mistakes made with customers.

_____ 35. When a mistake is made by our company, we are quick to offer an appropriate recovery.

_____ 36. We have a culture that is not afraid to say "I'm sorry" when it is appropriate.

_____ 37. We make it easy for customers to complain to us about our products and services.

_____ **Subtotal Section 7**


# Section 8: Responsiveness

_____ 38. We have a true sense of urgency when servicing our customers.

_____ 39. When we commit to a deadline, we do everything possible to achieve it.

_____ 40. When we tell someone, either internally or externally, that we will get back to them with some information, we do as we say.

_____ 41. When faced with unavoidable delays in our service delivery, we do what we can to communicate to the customer and minimize the inconvenience.

_____ 42. When problems with quality are identified, we take quick action to solve them.

_____ 43. We work hard to minimize the wait time for our customers.

_____ **Subtotal Section 8**


# Section 9: Teamwork

_____ 44. We have an organization that values teamwork.

_____ 45. Job descriptions and organizational boundaries are secondary to serving a customer.

_____ 46. We have a culture where team members look for ways to assist co-workers who are under pressure.

_____ 47. We have the opportunity to work on teams comprised of individuals in different departments to solve a problem or improve our services.

_____ 48. Leadership does a good job of sharing the credit for successes.

_____ 49. Employees feel they are involved in an exciting enterprise.

_____ 50. Employees are encouraged to discuss customer situations with leadership to make adjustments required to best meet the needs of the customer.

_____ **Subtotal Section 9**


## Section 10: Good, Better, Best!

_____ 51. We are not satisfied when things are simply good, but strive to do things in the best manner possible.

_____ 52. We are encouraged to always do more than is expected by our customers.

_____ 53. We strive to be a leader in our industry.

_____ 54. Our goal is to exceed the expectations of our customers in the things that matter most to them.

_____ **Subtotal Section 10**


## Section 11: Flexibility and Common Sense

_____ 55. Our policies and procedures make sense.

_____ 56. When an employee or customer questions a policy, any employee is capable of giving a logical explanation.

_____ 57. Employees at every level are empowered to use common sense when dealing with customer issues.

_____ 58. It is possible to modify a product or service based on trends in customer feedback.

_____ **Subtotal Section 11**


# Section 12: Respect the Customer

_____ 59. Senior leadership models a high level of respect for each other, employees and customers.

_____ 60. Employees are not permitted to ridicule or talk negatively about customers.

_____ 61. Disrespectful behaviors are dealt with promptly by leadership.

_____ **Subtotal Section 12**

## Totals

| | | | |
|---|---|---|---|
| _____ | Section 1 | _____ | Section 8 |
| _____ | Section 2 | _____ | Section 9 |
| _____ | Section 3 | _____ | Section 10 |
| _____ | Section 4 | _____ | Section 11 |
| _____ | Section 5 | _____ | Section 12 |
| _____ | Section 6 | | |
| _____ | Section 7 | _____ | **Grand Total** |

## Result Ranges

| | |
|---|---|
| 150+ | Your organization is doing a great job! |
| 120-149 | You understand the importance of customer service but need some help in the execution. |
| 90-119 | You get some of the concepts but generally have a lot of room for improvement. |
| less than 90 | Get some help or your organization may not exist next year! |

## About the Author

**David Reed** attended Texas A&M University where he received degrees in Chemical Engineering and Computer Science. Prior to founding Customer Centered Consulting Group, Inc., he served with Andersen Consulting, Exxon and Walt Disney World. David's mission is to utilize sound biblical principles to help organizations of all types and sizes improve their effectiveness by:

Getting the right **PEOPLE** (Human Resources) doing the
right **THINGS** (Operations) with the
right **ATTITUDE** (Customer Service) with the
right **TOOLS** (Technology) and for the
right **MONEY** (Finances).

David is also the author of two customer service books titled *Monday Morning Customer Service* and *Business Meets the Bible: Customer Service.* He conducts customer service training and consulting for a variety of organizations.

David resides in Frisco, Texas with his wife and two children. He travels throughout the country helping schools, churches, corporations and government agencies identify their strengths and weaknesses. Then, by working with leadership teams and teaching simple processes, he helps organizations create and implement common-sense solutions to their problems.

Well-known as a speaker and trainer in corporate America, David also has been a featured guest and expert on programs and panels exploring various customer-service issues.

David can be reached at 469.633.9833 or www.cccginc.com.

# Acknowledgments

*A Culture of Service* is dedicated to my wife, Heather, and my two children, Tony & Holly. They provide constant support and a reason for working hard each day.

My parents, Cal & Millie, for being available to read and proof my books and for supporting me throughout my career.

Thanks to David Cottrell and Melissa Monogue for using their talents to make these thoughts and concepts a reality through CornerStone Leadership Institute.

I am also thankful for the handful of companies that have developed their own culture of service and remind us all what it is like to receive excellent customer service. They keep the bar high and give everyone else something to shoot for.

A few of these exceptional companies that are constantly mentioned when I ask for examples of great service are:

> Disney
> Southwest Airlines
> Nordstrom
> Quick Trip Convenience Stores

And finally and most importantly, thank you to Jesus Christ for his sacrifice and giving me a roadmap to follow as I attempt to navigate through life. Without Him, life has no meaning.

# Accelerate Inspired Sales & Service Resources:

*Monday Morning Customer Service* takes you on a journey of eight lessons that demonstrate how to take care of customers so they keep coming back. **$14.95**

*Listen Up, Customer Service* is a step-by-step guide to improving customer relations while, at the same time, increasing employee satisfaction. **$9.95**

*You Gotta Get in the Game ... Playing to Win in Business, Sales and Life* provides direction on how to get into and win the game of life and business. **$14.95**

*Influential Selling – How to Win in Today's Selling Environment* is designed to stimulate new ways of thinking about your selling efforts and positioning them to align with your client. It will provide your team with new strategies and activities that will help you start winning today. **$14.95**

*180 Ways to Walk the Customer Service Talk* is packed with proven strategies and tips. This powerful handbook will get everyone "walking the customer service talk." **$9.95**

*Customer at the Crossroads* offers an entertaining way to reinforce key customer service values. It concludes with a series of thought-provoking questions, making it an effective vehicle for team discussions or reading groups. **$9.95**

*Orchestrating Attitude: Getting the Best from Yourself and Others* translates the abstract into the actionable. It cuts through the clutter to deliver inspiration and application so you can orchestrate your attitude ... and your success. **$9.95**

*Goal Setting for Results* addresses the fundamentals of setting and achieving your goal of moving yourself and your organization from where you are to where you want (and need) to be! **$9.95**

*The NEW CornerStone Perpetual Calendar*, a compelling collection of quotes about leadership and life, is perfect for office desks, school and home countertops. Offering a daily dose of inspiration, this terrific calendar makes the perfect gift or motivational reward. **$14.95**

*The CornerStone Leadership Collection of Cards* is designed to make it easy for you to show appreciation for your team, clients and friends. The awesome photography and your personal message written inside will create a lasting impact. Pack/12 (12 styles/1 each) **$24.95**
*Posters also available.*

Visit www.**CornerStoneLeadership**.com for
additional books and resources.

## ✔ YES! Please send me extra copies of *A Culture of Service!*
1-30 copies $14.95      31-100 copies $13.95      101+ copies $12.95

---

### *A Culture of Service*                    _____ copies X _____    = $ _____

---

### Additional Sales & Service Books

Accelerate Inspired Sales & Service Package       _____ pack(s) X $119.95    = $ _____
(Includes one copy of each product
listed on previous page.)

### Other Books

_____       _____ copies X _____    = $ _____

_____       _____ copies X _____    = $ _____

_____       _____ copies X _____    = $ _____

_____       _____ copies X _____    = $ _____

_____       _____ copies X _____    = $ _____

Shipping & Handling          $ _____

Subtotal          $ _____

Sales Tax (8.25%-TX Only)          $ _____

**Total (U.S. Dollars Only)**          $ _____

### Shipping and Handling Charges

| Total $ Amount | Up to $50 | $51-$99 | $100-$249 | $250-$1199 | $1200-$2999 | $3000+ |
|---|---|---|---|---|---|---|
| Charge | $6 | $9 | $16 | $30 | $80 | $125 |

Name _____ Job Title _____

Organization _____ Phone _____

Shipping Address _____ Fax _____

Billing Address _____ Email _____
(required when ordering PowerPoint® Presentation)

City _____ State _____ ZIP _____

❏ Please invoice (Orders over $200) Purchase Order Number (if applicable) _____

Charge Your Order:        ❏ MasterCard      ❏ Visa      ❏ American Express

Credit Card Number _____ Exp. Date _____

Signature _____

❏ Check Enclosed (Payable to: CornerStone Leadership)

**Mail**
**Phone  888.789.5323**                                                      **P.O. Box 764087**
**Fax  972.274.2884**          www.**CornerStoneLeadership**.com          **Dallas, TX 75376**

Thank you for reading *A Culture of Service!*
We hope it has assisted you in your quest for
personal and professional growth.

CornerStone Leadership is committed to provide new
and enlightening products to organizations worldwide.
Our mission is to fuel knowledge with practical resources
that will accelerate your team's productivity,
success and job satisfaction!

Best wishes for your continued success.

CornerStone
Leadership Institute
www.CornerStoneLeadership.com

*Start a crusade in your organization –
have the courage to learn, the vision to lead,
and the passion to share.*